HOW TO SAVE YOUR RELATIONSHIP

ANTHONY EKANEM

Contents

Preface

Even the happiest relationships go through troubled periods. Life is so full of change and uncertainties, and these can certainly put relationships to the test.

This book aims to help people who are facing difficulties in their relationships and need help with how to get things back on track. You may be considering if you even want to stay in the relationship at all. This book will help you consider your options and think everything through before walking away. Some of the ideas and techniques may even help you with other relationships in your life that you may have difficulties with – perhaps with a friend, parent, sibling, or other relatives.

CHAPTER ONE

Do You Both Want to Save It?

The fact that you are reading this book means that you care enough to get help with your relationship problems. However, a relationship takes more than one person to make it work. Both parties need to take responsibility for the relationship, and both need to also want to rebuild and save it.

What's your problem?

There are a million and one reasons why relationships go through difficulties. There may be external factors that have put pressure and stresses on your relationship – such as problems at work, a new baby, money, difficulties with other family members, etc. Infidelity could be another reason. There may not have been one incident, but a gradual build-up of resentment and bitterness over the years caused by smaller disagreements that have taken their toll on the relationship. The little things that you always saw as 'cute' and 'adorable' when you first got together now might grate on you intensely. It is interesting to note that traditionally infidelity has been the number one reason cited in divorce cases. However, according to a study by Grant Thornton in the UK, 'growing apart' and 'falling out of love' are now the most common reasons cited for divorce.

It is important to take some time to identify what the issues or problems are in your relationship. It is not a blame game; it is about being honest and both parties accepting responsibility on both sides. This can be a really difficult thing to do. Emotions may be charged and some things can be very difficult or painful to consider and indeed talk about. It is very much achievable to talk through these issues as a couple, but you may find that you need some professional help in coming to terms with these issues and need additional support with moving things forward.

Sometimes talking to someone impartial, whom neither of you knows, can help get some clarity in your relationship. Details of further help and support available are detailed at the end of this booklet.

Unrealistic expectations of your relationship?

So you've been together for quite some time. When you first got together, things were so exciting and your partner paid you lots of attention and showered you with gifts and love and affection. Things are not the same anymore. You can't help but look around at other couples walking down the street together, friends you know gushing about their other half, and telling you what a great relationship they have and have sex 3 times daily, happily ever after stories on film and TV.

Stop!!

Everyone feels like this from time to time in a relationship. It is quite normal. Things are not going to be the same as when you first got together. Things could be much better. That first flutter of giddy love and excitement does not and cannot last. What you have could be so much more than that. Excitement does not have to go out of the window, but your relationship grows into something else. Something more. A deeper and greater understanding, respect, and love for one another. Everyone's relationships are completely different. It is, after all, two different people with two different personalities. We all complement each other in different ways and what works for one relationship may not work for another. Because we are **all different**.

Take with a pinch of salt what others around you appear to be doing in their relationship. None ever knows what goes on inside someone else's relationship behind closed doors. Therefore it would be ridiculous to think that someone else's relationship is without problems and issues themselves and are better than your own.

If you hear from a friend that they are having intercourse with their partner three times a week and you are having sexual intercourse once every month, every few months, or even once a year, this does not matter. There is no 'normal' frequency for how often couples have sex. Love does not necessarily go hand in hand with the act of sexual intercourse. The important thing is that you are both happy with the frequency of sex in your relationship. If you are both happy with doing it once a year then that's great! Equally if one of you wants to do it every night and the other once a year, then there is a problem. You are not sexually compatible and will need to consider how you move forward with this in your relationship.

CHAPTER TWO

Putting the Past to Rest

Hurtful things that have been said and done in the past: infidelity, disappointment and bitterness felt by actions taken by your partner. These are all difficult things that can be experienced in a relationship and they can be even more difficult to get over. Unfortunately, you cannot have a brain autopsy and forget but you can leave these things in the past and move forward with your future. You can never forget but you can forgive. With good communication with your partner and professional support, if needed, you can learn to put the past to rest and move on.

It may be that there is an issue that even by talking through with each other, you come to no resolution over. Sometimes you have to 'agree to disagree' and move forward. Even loving couples cannot agree on everything and being able to overlook certain things is essential for the survival of any relationship.

Are we compatible?

For any relationship to last, you must be compatible. This does not mean that you have to share all of each other's hobbies and interests and live in each other's pockets. It could be considered unhealthy if you do. The happiest people in the most successful relationships give each other space and time to follow other interests away from the relationship. You are, after all, two separate people with two separate personalities and interests. The important thing is that you can come back together and enjoy each other's company and pursue other interests that you may share.

Being compatible with someone is being able to work well together. It is about having similar outlooks on life, sharing a similar sense of humour, and wanting similar things.

Consider the following questions within your relationship. Indicate where you feel your relationship rates on a scale of 1 to 10 for each question (1 being the least and 10 being the most). Try to think about each question in terms of your feelings over the last month or so rather than just how you are feeling today:

1. **Sex:** How sexually fulfilled do you feel? Are you happy with the frequency of sex in your relationship?

1. **Fun:** Sense of humour. Shared interests. How much do you laugh together?

3. **Shared values:** Do you have a similar philosophy of life and moral code?

4. **Common goals:** Are you heading in the same direction? Do you want the same things or is there room for compromise?

5. **Social life:** Friends and family. How happy are you with the level and quality of interaction you have with them?

6. **Conflict resolution:** How well do you both manage disagreements? Do you respect each other's boundaries? Are you able to ask for what you need?

7. **Communication:** Do you know what's going on in each other's life, and are you both interested?

8. **Chores:** How happy are you both with the way chores are shared?

9. **Emotional support:** How supportive is your partner, especially in times of stress and illness?

10. **Career support:** How supportive is your partner of your career or other aspirations?

What you need to do next!

Add up your scores. This will be out of a total of 100. Please note that a score of 100 is completely unrealistic. If you have scored 70 or more, it can be suggested that you and your partner are compatible but may still want to look at the areas where you scored less than 7.

The aim of this exercise is not to give you an overall score of whether you should leave your relationship or not, but to give you some indication of your compatibility with one another and areas that you may want to investigate a bit more. It may also give you some comfort that in some areas where you have scored more highly, then that aspect of your relationship is working well. Take some encouragement from that. For example, maybe you have scored low on the sex question. This is an area that you can discuss with your partner and look at ways of coming to some compromise. However, at the same time, you might have scored your relationship a '9' for the fun you have together and how often you laugh. You know that this is a strength in your relationship and are still compatible in that area.

It is worth letting your partner score your relationship on the same set of questions also. This will see if you are singing on the same hymn sheet and finding the same problems in your relationship. It may be that there is an area that you find problematic in your relationship and your partner had no idea and they viewed things are being fine in that area. It is no wonder that this would develop itself as a problem. But now your partner knows how you feel about it, you can work on this and move forward.

CHAPTER THREE

Communication in the Relationship

Once you have considered your compatibility, to move forward with rebuilding your relationship, you must spend time together to talk about issues and problems that you face in your relationship. This can be so difficult, especially when emotions are running high. Try to pick a time when you are both as relaxed as possible. Agree that this is a time when you will not raise your voice or argue. Make sure it is at a time when you will not be disturbed and not on your way out the door. This cannot be rushed.

Listening is just as important as talking. There are two sides to everything in life and you must give your partner as much opportunity to communicate their feelings and take on things as you do with them. You may not have realised why your partner feels, says, and does certain things before and this is an opportunity for you to gain some understanding and vice versa.

It is unlikely that all problems in your relationship will be resolved in one sitting, but this will be a good starting point in helping you both get things back on track. If there is more than one issue, talk about it one at a time. Agree to come back together in the next few days to talk some more. Put it in your diary. Talking to each other calmly and respecting each other's viewpoints by listening will help your relationship greatly. As I previously said, this can be very difficult to do on your own. Don't be afraid to get some professional support to help you both rebuild your relationship.

Invest time and effort into your relationship.

People invest so much time into their jobs and careers, children, and even household chores! It is equally as important to invest as much time and effort as you can into your relationship. This can be difficult when you have got a hundred and one things to do and fit in every day – but is essential that you do! Even half an hour a day, or even every few days, to stop doing everything else and sit down together and talk.

The talking does not need to be deep and meaningful – even just a catch-up on how your day has been. It is so easy to lose touch with each other as each day passes, and you end up living like strangers. Bring things back to basics. Get to know each other again. There is no rush; take it slowly. Perhaps go on a date together once a week or even once a month. Put it in your diaries. Do not be tempted to discuss your potential split on the date itself. Talk about other things in your life. Talk about things that brought you together in the first place. Don't feel the date has to end up going to bed together. Again, take things slowly. You are beginning again, and new rules apply!

CHAPTER FOUR

When It's Time to Let Go

If you are in an abusive relationship, physically or emotionally, it may be best to leave and find a fresh start. However, no one can tell you what to do. Only you can decide. It is important to look after yourself though and consider the effects of your relationship on any children you have.

As long as both parties want to make the relationship work, there is always hope. If things have changed in your relationship, things can always change back – or change in another different way – for the better! If your partner accepts no responsibility for the problems in your relationship and is unwilling to work with you to repair your relationship, unfortunately, there is little you can do. You do only have one life after all, and you need to consider whether it is worth continuing to fight a battle that may have already been lost. Equally, if your partner tells you that they do not want to make it work unfortunately there is nothing you can do but let them go. No begging or pleading can save a relationship. If the relationship has come to an end, get as much support as you can - from friends and relatives and if necessary, from professionals. You may feel that you do not need only emotional support but also practical and financial advice. Check out your legal rights.

You can do this without cost by consulting the Citizens Advice Bureau or cheaply by asking a solicitor for a fixed-fee interview. This doesn't mean you are starting divorce proceedings; it simply means you are finding out where you stand. Don't assume that because the house or mortgage is in your partner's name you have no share in it and don't believe them if they say they won't pay maintenance. There are rules about these things and your legal adviser can explain them.

Remember, a loving and lasting relationship is about:

- Listening
- Overlooking
- Valuing
- Everlasting